D1365697

PRACTICAL COMPANIONS

Herb Gardener

by LINDA TSIRICOS

Illustrated by ANNY EVASON

Contents

CHAPTER ONE
Herbs in History

Folk Medicine—An Oral Tradition

The discovery of a Neanderthal grave in Iraq, which revealed the seeds of seven plants that are still recognized for their medicinal properties today, leaves little doubt that the tradition of herbal medicine is as old as mankind itself. Early hunter-gatherers must have discovered, at first by trial and error, not only that some plants tasted pleasant while others were bitter and unpalatable but also that some made them feel ill, or proved fatal in some cases, while others seemed to cure their ailments and give them strength.

The ancient Aztec and Maya civilizations in Mexico practiced herbalism in conjunction with astrology and in Peru the Incas used many plants that are still used today to treat the same illnesses; they are known to have used quinine to reduce fevers, and to treat digestive disorders.

In North America, each tribe of Native Americans had its medicine man who was both herbalist and spiritual healer. Some tribes believed that evil spirits invaded the body and caused disease, and could only be driven out by the bitter herbal concoctions that the medicine man administered. Some thought that, without spiritual guidance, the medicine man could not select the appropriate remedies, while others believed that the plants' medicinal properties were bestowed upon them by benign spirits, who then became the plants' guardians.

The ancient tradition of Ayurvedic healing, which is based on the use of 700 different herbs, is still practiced today in the Indian sub-continent and in Asian communities abroad. Many Ayurvedic remedies are a type of aromatherapy, with the treatment being administered in the form of essential oils which are massaged into the skin.

For thousands of years, mankind's ever-increasing knowledge of the role that herbs could play in improving his quality of life and general well-being was passed down only by word of mouth from generation to generation. It was not until around 2700BC that the Chinese Emperor Shen Nung listed 350 herbs and their properties in the *Pharmacopoeia of the Heavenly Husbandman* and a new chapter in the history of herbal medicines began to unfold.

The Great Herbalists

By 2000BC, the Ancient Egyptians were keeping detailed accounts on papyrus scrolls of prescriptions for the treatment of a vast number of illnesses and disorders, as well as formulas for the preparation of cosmetics and embalming fluids. Many of the herbs, spices, and essential oils used in these preparations were imported from Babylon, and some were brought from as far away as India.

Hippocrates, who is regarded by many as the "Father of Medicine," opened the world's first medical school in Greece around 400BC, and, by the end of the 1st century AD, Dioscorides, a Greek physician employed by the Roman army, had compiled *De Materia Medica*, a vast encyclopedia of medicine.

The Roman Empire spread not only its knowledge of herbal medicine across Europe, but also the herbs themselves. An essential part of every Roman soldier's kit was the seeds of plants that he could grow to replenish his "medicine chests." Many of the herbs, such as sage (*Salvia officinalis*), borage (*Borago officinalis*), and thyme (*Thymus vulgaris*), that now grow wild in Britain, were carefully cultivated by the Roman legions.

With the establishment of Christianity in Britain came the monasteries in whose gardens a great variety of herbs were cultivated. These provided the monks with ingredients from which they prepared lotions, tinctures, and ointments to treat the local population. The monasteries quickly came to be regarded as something akin to present-day clinics. By the Middle Ages, folk remedies were common throughout the country, and in rural areas, where illiteracy was the norm, the oral tradition of herbalism survived for many years alongside the written works of the physicians and scholars.

The first scientific study of plants was published in the middle of the 16th century in William Turner's *New Herball*, but it was not until the end of the century that John Gerard, an apothecary to King James I of England, produced a *Herball* that included plants from the "new lande" of America. Much that Gerard wrote was contradicted by the physician Nicholas Culpeper in his *Herball* of 1653, but Culpeper's work was discredited by many, who considered it to be unscholarly and astrological rather than scientific.

Nicholas Monardes, a Spanish doctor after whom *Monarda didyma* (Oswego tea) was named, made a study of herbs in the "New World," and in 1569 he wrote what is believed to be the first American herbal, *Joyfull Newes Out of the Newe Founde Worlde*. Many settlers had brought seeds and roots of their culinary and medicinal herbs from the "Old World" and these quickly established themselves alongside the indigenous species, which included Oswego tea and evening primrose (*Oenothera biennis*), that were already widely used by the native Americans.

Monardes' book was followed in 1672 by John Josselyn's *New England's Rarities Discover'd*. Josselyn made a detailed study of plants to establish which European ones were best suited to cultivation in America. His writings were intended to give gardening advice to the settlers, who were unfamiliar with the climate and soil conditions in their new surroundings.

Swedish botanist, Carl Linnaeus, was instrumental in turning the study of plant life into a science. In 1737 he devised a system of plant classification and established the use of botanical Latin as a universal method of plant identification. He began by grouping plants into different

classes, determined by their structural characteristics. He then sub-divided each genus into individual species which distinguished each plant from the others in the same genus. Many changes have been made to Linnaeus' original classifications, but his work remains the foundation of modern botany.

The middle of the 18th century saw an increase in the popularity of herbs and herbal medicine in America. This was largely due to the Shakers, whose belief in the benefits of simple living and small-scale agriculture led them to become the first settlers to trade commercially in home-grown herbs and herbal products on a relatively large scale.

In Europe, meanwhile, where the climate, particularly in the south, encouraged the growth of healthy, vigorous plants, the large-scale commercial production of herbs for both culinary and medicinal purposes was already established and has continued ever since. In the countries of Northern Europe, however, where the growth of many herbs is less prolific, due to lower average temperatures and higher rain-fall, their popularity gradually decreased and by the time of the Industrial Revolution, their use in Britain had all but died out.

How Did Their Gardens Grow?

It is impossible to determine at what point in history man first moved plants from the wild to cultivate them in a place that he, rather than nature, had chosen. We will never know if the first garden was the pride and joy of a cave dweller or of someone who lived thousands of years later, but there is no doubt that by 2000BC herb gardens were widespread in ancient Egypt. The Egyptians used herbs, such as frankincense (*Boswellia sacra*) and myrrh (*Commiphora myrrah*), and other sacred plants in the worship of their gods and in the embalming of their dead. To ensure that only the best and freshest plants were used, the gardens were usually close to their temples.

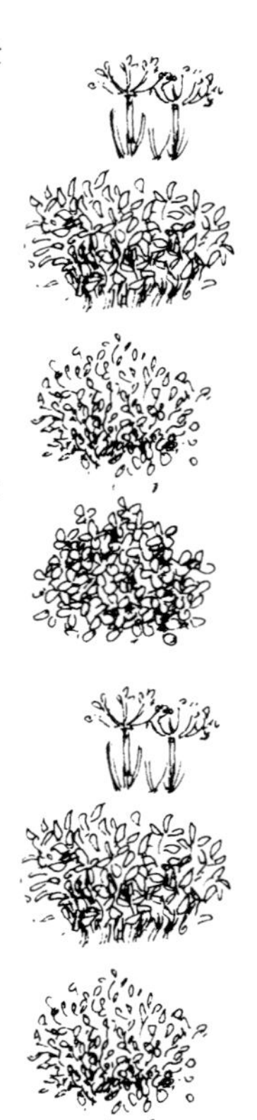

Roman herb gardens, like the villas they surrounded, were geometric in their design. They consisted of a series of formal beds, often surrounded by small hedges, which accommodated medicinal, culinary, and aromatic herbs, such as bay (*Laurus nobilis*), rosemary (*Rosemarinus officinalis*) and thyme.

The early Christian monasteries perpetuated the same style as the Romans, but often on a larger scale, where enough herbs, vegetables, and fruit could be grown to ensure self-sufficiency for the monks and provide ingredients for herbal medicines to administer to the sick.

Physic gardens were a development of the 16th century and were created by universities for the purpose of teaching medicine and botany to their students. The herbs were carefully laid out in the gardens, often in alphabetical order, and planted in ways that allowed easy access for close inspection by the students. The first physic garden was opened at the University of Padua, in Italy, in 1545 and by the end of the 17th century almost every university in Europe had one. Many of these physic gardens grew and developed into today's botanic gardens.

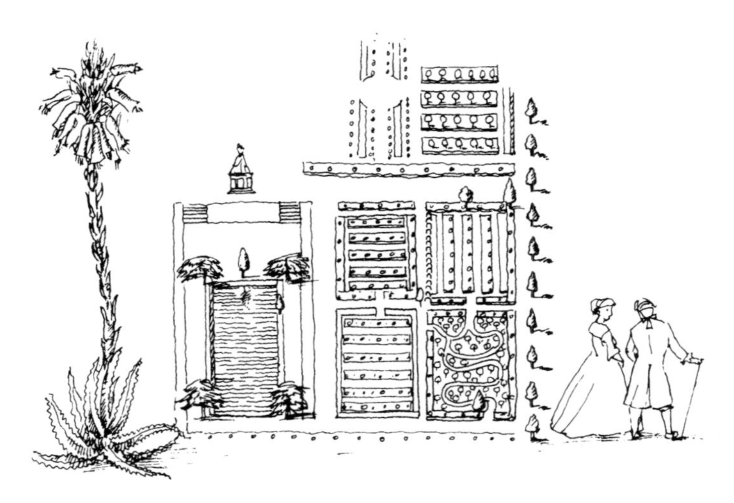

More recently, changing fashions rather than functionality have dictated garden styles, and herbs have been grown in every setting from the knot gardens of Elizabethan England to vast formal potagers such as those at the Chateau Villandry in France, to the tiny cottage gardens of countryfolk, where herbs flourished side by side with vegetables and fruit in glorious disarray.

ALLIUM
SCHOENOPRASUM
FOENICULUM
VULGARE
ROSEMARINUS
OFFICINALIS
LAURUS
NOBILIS
OCIMUM
BASILICUM

CHAPTER TWO

Choosing Your Herbs

When you buy herbs, or any other plant, always use the botanical (Latin) name for what you want. That way you will avoid the shock of seeing what you expected to be a delicate, sweetly scented herb rapidly grow into an enormous bush that threatens to take over your garden. The common names for plants vary from country to country, and even from state to state. *Lunaria*, which Americans call "silver dollar plants," are known in England as "honesty" and as "silver pennies" in Scotland. Using the botanical names for plants leaves no room for misunderstandings, and whether you buy in Boston, Bengal, or Beijing, you should return home with the plant you want.

Among the herbs listed, some are best known for their aromatic or decorative qualities, some for their culinary uses, and others for their medicinal or cosmetic properties. Whatever your reasons for growing herbs, I hope you'll find some here that will inspire you to create an herb garden of your own.

Angelica (Angelica archangelica)
Hardy biennial

Height/spread: 6 x 3ft (2 x 1m).
Description: Bright green aromatic leaves; creamy white flowers in summer.
Position: Deep, moist soil in partial shade.
Cultivation: Sow in situ in late summer; thin out to 3ft (1m) apart in spring.
Harvest: Young stems in early summer; leaves before flowering; seeds in late fall; roots at end of first year. 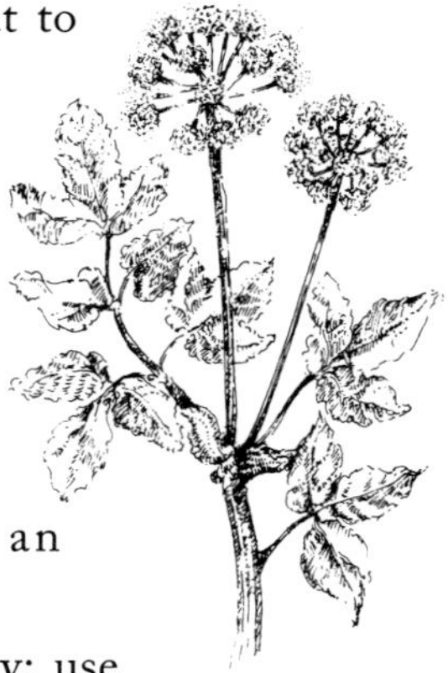
USES:
Aromatic/decorative: Add leaves to potpourri. Include seed heads in dried flower arrangements.
Cosmetic: Add leaves to bath water for an invigorating bath.
Culinary: Stew leaves with fruit to reduce acidity; use seeds to add flavor to drinks; candy (crystallize) stems for cake decoration.
Medicinal: Infuse leaves to treat colds and flatulence; hang a sachet of crushed, dried leaves in the car to reduce travel sickness.

*A*NISE *(Pimpinella anisum)*
Annual

Height/spread: 20 x 10-18in (50 x 25-45cm).
Description: Mid-green, aromatic lower leaves, feathery upper leaves; small, star-shaped, white flowers in late summer.
Position: Poor, dry, alkaline soil; sunny and sheltered.
Cultivation: Sow in situ in late spring; thin to 6in (15cm) apart in summer.
Aftercare: Keep surrounding soil weed free.
Harvest: Lower leaves when needed; flowers as they open; seeds as they begin to turn grayish-green.
USES:
Aromatic/decorative: Add crushed seeds to potpourri.
Cosmetic: Add ground seeds to mud packs (face packs) to lighten freckles. Chew toasted seeds to sweeten the breath.
Culinary: Whole or ground seeds add flavour to apple pies, breads, cakes, cookies, and curries. Add fresh, chopped leaves to vegetable or fruit salads.
Household/garden: Seeds attract mice—sprinkle them on cheese in mousetraps.

Basil (Ocimum basilicum) Bush basil / Greek basil, (O.b. var. *minimum)* Tender annual

Height/spread: Sweet basil 18 x 6in (45 x 15cm), bush basil 6 x 12in (15 x 30cm).
Description: Sweet basil–large, bright green, clove-scented leaves; small, white, aromatic flowers in late summer. Bush basil–small, pale green leaves; tiny, white flowers in summer.
Position: Light, rich, well-drained soil in full sun.
Cultivation: Sow thinly indoors in spring; plant out sweet basil 8in (20cm) apart, bush basil 14in (35cm) apart when all danger of frost is past.
Aftercare: Spray leaves in hot weather; pinch out growing tips to encourage bushy growth.
Harvest: Leaves as flowers begin to open.
Uses:
Cosmetic: Add leaves to bath water for a refreshing bath.
Culinary: Tear leaves into salads and tomato dishes. Main ingredient of pesto sauce.
Household/garden: Grow indoors in pots to deter flies.
Medicinal: Infuse leaves to aid digestion and relieve stomach cramps and nausea.

BAY (*Laurus nobilis*)
Evergreen tree

Height/spread: Up to 40 x 40ft (12 x 12m), but usually grown as a bush.
Description: Dark green, glossy, aromatic leaves; creamy yellow flowers, followed by small, purple fruits in fall.
Position: Rich, moist, well-drained soil; sunny and sheltered.
Cultivation: Plant 4ft (1.2m) apart in warm climates. Best grown in containers in colder areas. Propagate by semiripe cuttings in late summer.
Aftercare: Protect from frost.
Harvest: Leaves when needed.
USES:
Aromatic/decorative: Crumble dried leaves into potpourri. Trees make good subjects for topiary.
Cosmetic: Add decoction of leaves to bath water.
Culinary: Use in bouquet garni. One or two fresh or dried leaves enhance the flavor of most dishes. Remove before serving.
Household/garden: Add a leaf to flour to deter weevils.

BORAGE (*Borago officinalis*)
Hardy annual

Height/spread: 24 x 16in (60 x 40cm).
Description: Grayish-green, prickly, cucumber-flavored leaves; sky blue, star-shaped flowers in summer.
Position: Light, poor, chalky or sandy soil in sun.
Cultivation: Sow in situ in spring for summer flowers, in fall for spring flowers; thin to 24in (60cm) apart. Self-seeds freely.
Harvest: Leaves when needed; flowers when fully open.
USES:
Aromatic/decorative: Thread flowers together to make pretty necklaces for children.
Cosmetic: Add leaves to mud packs to treat dry skin.
Culinary: Sprinkle flowers in salads; candy for cake decoration; add finely chopped young leaves to salads, or cook like spinach.
Household/garden: Grow with strawberries. Each will stimulate growth of the other.
Medicinal: Leaves are rich in mineral salts and suitable for salt-free diets.

CARAWAY (Carum carvi)
Hardy biennial

Height/spread: 24 x 12in (60 x 30cm).
Description: Feathery leaves; tiny, white flowers in summer.
Position: Light, well-drained soil in full sun.
Cultivation: Sow in situ in late spring or early fall; thin to 8in (20cm) apart.
Aftercare: Protect roots of young plants with a mulch in winter.
Harvest: Leaves when young; seed heads when brown, but before they open.
USES:
Aromatic/decorative: Add crushed seeds to potpourri.
Culinary: Use seeds to flavor apple pies, breads, cakes, cookies and cheese. Add chopped leaves to salads and soups.
Medicinal: Chew raw seeds to promote appetite and sweeten the breath. Infuse leaves to relieve flatulence and stimulate appetite. Safe for babies with colic.
~ Caraway can be grown indoors.

CATNIP / CATMINT (Nepeta cataria)
Hardy herbaceous perennial

Height/spread: 20 x 16in (50 x 40cm).
Description: Soft, grayish-green, aromatic leaves; white, purple-spotted flowers from summer to mid fall.
Position: Fertile, well-drained soil in sun or partial shade.
Cultivation: Sow in spring; thin to 12in (30cm) apart. Propagate by softwood cuttings in late spring.
Aftercare: Cut back plants in fall.
Harvest: Leaves when young; flowering tops as they develop.
USES:
Aromatic/decorative: Add crushed, dried leaves to potpourri.
Culinary: Rub fresh leaves on lamb before roasting. Add to mint sauce for extra flavor.
Household/garden: Use dried leaves to stuff toy mice for cats. Grow near vegetables to deter flea beetles.
Medicinal: Infuse leaves to relieve colds and induce sleep; crush leaves and flowering tops to make a poultice for bruises.
❧ Cats find catnip irresistible and will roll on the plants. Protect young plants with wire mesh until established.

CHAMOMILE (*Chamaemelum nobile*)
Hardy evergreen perennial

Height/spread: 8-12 x 4-6in (20-30 x 10-15cm).
Description: Bright green, feathery, apple-scented leaves; aromatic, white, daisylike flowers with golden centers in summer and fall.

Position: Light, well-drained, slightly acid soil in full sun.
Cultivation: Sow in situ in spring; thin to 9in (23cm) apart. Self-seeds freely.
Harvest: Leaves when needed; flowers when fully open.
USES:
Aromatic/decorative: Add dried flowers and leaves to pot-pourri and herb pillows. A vase of fresh flowers makes a simple, fragrant, summer display.
Cosmetic: Infuse flowers to rinse and condition fair hair, to use as mouthwash, and to bathe tired, inflamed eyes.
Medicinal: Infuse flowers for a general tonic and sedative; safe to give to children at bedtime to induce sleep and prevent nightmares; add to bath water to relieve sunburn.
❧ Chamomile grows well in containers.

CHERVIL (Anthriscus cerefolium)
Hardy biennial

Height/spread: 18 x 12in (45 x 30cm).
Description: Light green, lacy leaves; clusters of tiny, white flowers in late spring or summer.
Position: Light, well-drained soil in partial shade.
Cultivation: Sow monthly in spring, summer, and fall; thin to 6-9in (15-23cm) apart. Does not transplant successfully.
Aftercare: For a supply of leaves in winter, protect plants with plastic covers.
Harvest: Outside leaves before plants flower.
USES:
Cosmetic: Infuse leaves to make skin cleanser.
Culinary: Use chopped leaves in chicken, egg and white fish dishes, salads and sauces, and to make chervil soup. For best flavor, add leaves near the end of the cooking time.
Medicinal: High in vitamin C, beta carotene, iron, and magnesium. Infuse leaves to stimulate digestion and improve circulation. Ingredient of *fines herbes.*
❧ Chervil quickly runs to seed in hot climates.
a

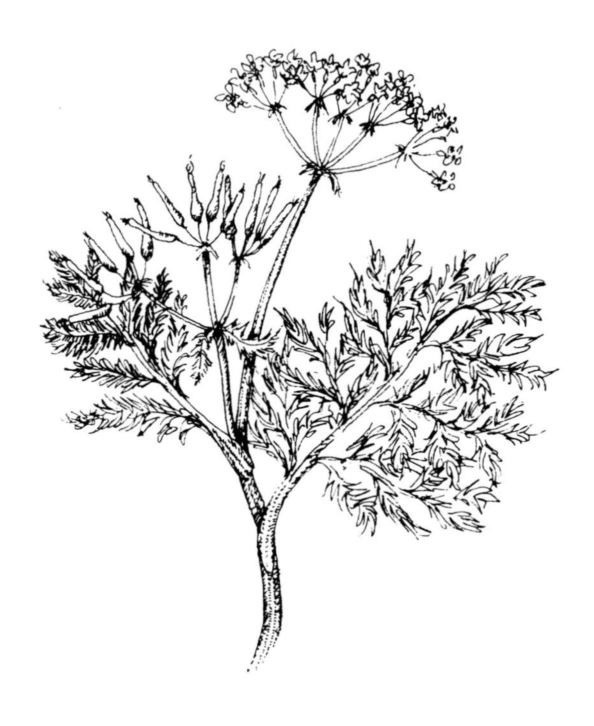

Chives (Allium schoenoprasum)
Hardy perennial

Height/spread: 12-15 x 6in (30-40 x 15cm).
Description: Long, thin leaves, round mauve flowers in summer.
Position: Moist, well-drained soil in sun.
Cultivation: Sow in situ in spring; thin to 12in (30cm) apart. Divide clumps in fall or spring.
Aftercare: Remove flower buds to increase flavor of leaves. Keep well watered.
Harvest: Cut to 2in (5cm) above ground. Pick flowers as they open.
USES:
Aromatic/decorative: Plants make attractive edging for flower borders.
Culinary: Sprinkle florets on salads. Add chopped leaves to cream cheese, salads, sandwiches, stir-fries, and soups.
Household/garden: Grow near fruit trees to deter aphids, apple scab, and mildew.
Medicinal: Stimulates appetite and aids digestion. Mildly laxative.
❧ Chives can be grown indoors.

COMFREY / KNITBONE (*Symphytum officinale*)
Hardy herbaceous perennial

Height/spread: 24-36 x 12in (60-90 x 30cm).
Description: Large, rough, slightly prickly, dark green leaves; mauve, bell-shaped flowers in summer.
Position: Nitrogen-rich soil in full sun.
Cultivation: Grow from root cuttings planted 2ft (60cm) apart, anytime except midwinter.
Aftercare: Mulch with well-rotted compost or manure in late spring.
Harvest: Leaves in midsummer, roots in late fall.
USES:
Cosmetic: Infuse leaves and roots to add to bath water to relieve aching joints.
Culinary: Cook leaves like spinach.
Household/garden: Soak leaves in water to make a liquid fertilizer for tomatoes; add to compost heap to accelerate decomposition.
Medicinal: Apply a poultice of fresh leaves to aching joints and fractures. Infuse leaves and roots to treat stomach ulcers. Spread leaves on cuts and open wounds.

CORIANDER *(Coriandrum sativum)*
Hardy annual

Height/spread: 24 x 6in (60 x 15cm).
Description: Aromatic, broad, lower leaves, feathery upper leaves; whitish pink flowers in early summer.
Position: Rich, well-drained soil in full sun.
Cultivation: Sow in situ, in fall in warm climates, early spring in colder regions; thin to 4-6in (10-15cm) apart.
Harvest: Young leaves when needed; seeds when plump and beginning to change color.
USES:
Aromatic/decorative: Add whole or ground seeds to potpourri.
Culinary: Use ground or whole seeds in curries and pork dishes. Add leaves to curries, salads, and sauces.
Medicinal: Chew fresh leaves or drink infusion to stimulate appetite and aid digestion.
❧ Coriander will reduce fennel's ability to produce seeds if these plants are grown too close together.

DILL *(Anethum graveolens)*
Hardy annual

Height/spread: 24 x 24in (60 x 60cm).
Description: Aromatic, lacy, bluish-green leaves; tiny, very aromatic, yellow flowers in summer.
Position: Rich, well-drained soil; sunny and sheltered.
Cultivation: Sow in situ in spring in cool climates, in fall in warmer regions; thin to 9-12in (23-30cm) apart. Self-seeds freely.
Harvest: Leaves when young, seeds when plump and beginning to change color.
USES:
Cosmetic: Infuse crushed seeds to strengthen nails.
Culinary: Use whole or ground seeds in apple pies, breads, butter, cabbage, dill pickle, and fish dishes. Add finely chopped leaves to broiled (grilled) meats, cream cheese, egg dishes, potato salad, and salmon.
Medicinal: Infuse seeds to relieve colic, hiccups, indigestion, insomnia, and stomach cramps. Safe treatment for babies, to relieve colic and induce sleep.
❧ Grow dill away from fennel or they will cross-pollinate and the flavor of both plants will be spoiled.

Fennel (Foeniculum vulgare)
Hardy herbaceous perennial

Height/spread: 4 x 3ft (1.2 x 1m).
Description: Lime green, feathery, very aromatic leaves; small, yellow, aromatic flowers in midsummer.
Position: Moderately rich, well-drained soil in full sun.
Cultivation: Sow in situ in early spring; thin to 20in (50cm) apart. Self-seeds freely once established.
Harvest: Stems and leaves when needed; seeds when ripe.
USES:
Cosmetic: Chew seeds to freshen breath; decoct to bathe inflamed eyes. Add seeds and leaves to facial steams and bath water.
Culinary: Use leaves to garnish fish; chop and add to pork dishes, salads, and soups. Chop young stems into salads. Use seeds in breads, fish dishes, and sauces.
Medicinal: Infuse seeds to aid digestion.
❧ Grow fennel away from dill, otherwise they will cross-pollinate and the flavors of both will be spoiled. Coriander grown near fennel reduces the production of fennel seeds.

Feverfew (Tanacetum parthenium)
Hardy perennial

Height/spread: 24 x 18in (60 x 45cm).
Description: Yellowish green, aromatic leaves; small, daisylike flowers with white petals and yellow centers in summer.
Position: Dry, well-drained soil in sun or partial shade.
Cultivation: Sow in spring or fall; thin to 12in (30cm) apart. Self-seeds freely.
Harvest: Leaves and flowers anytime.
USES:
Aromatic/decorative: Dried flowers add color to potpourri.
Household/garden: Place sachets of dried leaves in linen drawers and closets or wardrobes to deter moths.
Medicinal: Eat leaves in sandwiches to relieve migraine. Mildly laxative.
~ Feverfew can be grown indoors in a cool place.

French tarragon (Artemesia dracunculus)
Half-hardy perennial

Height/spread: 36 x 16in (90 x 40cm).
Description: Long, narrow, shiny, aromatic leaves; tiny, greenish white flowers which open fully only in warm climates.
Position: Rich, light, dry soil; sunny and sheltered.
Cultivation: Plant 12-18in (30-45cm) apart. Propagate by dividing in spring, or take stem cuttings in summer. Does not set seed in temperate climates.
Aftercare: Feed with organic fertilizer throughout growing season. Cut back in fall. Protect with straw mulch in winter, or grow in containers and take indoors.
Harvest: Leaves when needed, but best in late summer.
USES:
Culinary: Add shredded leaves to omelets, mayonnaise, salad dressings, and scrambled eggs; rub on chicken skin before roasting or add to stuffing; sprinkle over fish before baking.
Medicinal: Rich in vitamins A and C and iodine and mineral salts. Infuse leaves as a tonic and appetite stimulant.

Garlic (*Allium sativum*)
Hardy perennial

Height/spread: 18-24 x 4in (45-60 x 10cm).
Description: Flat leaves; white flowers in summer.
Position: Moist, well-drained soil in sun or partial shade.
Cultivation: Plant individual cloves 2in (5cm) deep, 6in (15cm) apart in fall or early spring.
Aftercare: Remove flower buds as they appear. Keep well watered.
Harvest: Lift bulbs gently in late summer when foliage dies down.
Uses:
Culinary: Use chopped or crushed cloves in salads, sauces, and stews, and to flavor butter; add to pan when frying eggs or mushrooms.
Household/garden: Grow under peach trees to control leaf curl and near roses to enhance their fragrance.
Medicinal: Antibiotic. Take internally to treat bronchitis, catarrh, colds, and whooping cough, and to reduce blood pressure. Apply to the skin as a remedy for acne and athlete's foot.

Horehound (Marrubium vulgare)
Hardy perennial

Height/spread: 18 x 18in (45 x 45cm).
Description: Wrinkled grayish green leaves covered in white down; small, white flowers in summer and fall.
Position: Dry, neutral to alkaline soil; sunny and sheltered.
Cultivation: Sow in situ in spring; thin to 12in (30cm) apart. Propagate by stem cuttings in late spring.
Aftercare: Do not allow roots to become waterlogged in winter.
Harvest: Leaves and flowers when needed.
USES:
Aromatic/decorative: Include in dried flower arrangements.
Household/garden: Infuse leaves in milk to kill house flies.
Medicinal: Mix chopped leaves with honey to ease sore throats. Make tincture to treat coughs.
~ Horehound is attractive to bees.

LADY'S MANTLE (Alchemilla vulgaris)
Hardy herbaceous perennial

Height/spread: 6-20 x 6in (15-50 x 15cm).
Description: Soft, round, bluish-green leaves; greenish yellow flowers in summer.
Position: Rich, moist, alkaline soil in sun or partial shade.
Cultivation: Sow in spring or fall; thin to 2ft (60cm) apart. Propagate by dividing in spring or fall. Self-seeds freely.
Harvest: Large leaves while plant is in flower.
USES:
Aromatic/decorative: Attractive when grown in hanging baskets.
Cosmetic: Infuse dried leaves for a facial steam to treat acne; use to bathe inflamed eyes.
Culinary: Tear young leaves into salads.
Household/garden: Boil leaves to make green dye for wool.
Medicinal: Infuse leaves to cure diarrhea and to regulate menstruation.

LAVENDER (Lavandula angustifolia)
Hardy evergreen shrub

Height/spread: 18-36 x 24in (45-100 x 30cm) depending on variety.
Description: Narrow, aromatic, grayish green leaves; small, purple, pink, or white, highly scented flowers in summer.
Position: Well-drained, sandy soil in sun.
Cultivation: Sow in late summer or fall; thin to 18-24in (45-60cm) apart. Propagate by stem cuttings, or dividing or layering.

Lavandula augustifolia "Munstead"

Aftercare: Remove faded flower stems. Prune in late fall. Protect from strong winds in winter.
Harvest: Flower stems as flowers begin to open.
USES:
Aromatic/decorative: Use dried flowers in herb pillows and scented sachets; add dried flowers and leaves to potpourri. Include flowers in fresh or dried arrangements. Makes attractive, aromatic hedge.

Lavandula stoechas

Cosmetic: Infuse flowers to make lotion to treat acne.
Culinary: Candy fresh flowers or add to ice cream, jams, and vinegar.
Household/garden: Place sachets of dried flowers in drawers and closets to repel moths.
Medicinal: Infuse flowers to ease headaches, to combat dizziness and fainting, and to induce sleep. Safe treatment for hyperactive children.

Lavandula angustifolia "Hidcote"

Lavandula x *intermedia*

Lemon Balm (Melissa officinalis)
Hardy herbaceous perennial

Height/spread: 18-24 x 16-24in (45-60 x 40-60cm).
Description: Light green, hairy, lemon-scented leaves; small, yellow flowers in summer.
Position: Rich, moist soil in partial shade.
Cultivation: Sow in spring; thin to 12in (30cm) apart. Self-seeds freely.
Harvest: Leaves as flowers begin to open.
Uses:
Aromatic/decorative: Add dried leaves to potpourri.
Cosmetic: Infuse leaves for a facial steam and a rinse for oily hair.
Culinary: Chop leaves into fresh fruit or vegetable salads; add to stuffings for lamb, pork, and poultry.
Household/garden: Crush leaves and add juice to furniture polish.
Medicinal: Apply fresh leaves to insect bites and stings. Infuse leaves to relieve headaches and fatigue.
❧ Lemon balm is attractive to bees, but can be very invasive and needs kept within bounds.

LEMON VERBENA (Aloysia triphylla)
Half-hardy shrub

Height/spread: Up to 10 x 10ft (3 x 3m).
Description: Lemon-scented leaves; tiny, white and lilac flowers in late summer.
Position: Poor, dry, alkaline soil; sunny and sheltered. Frost-free site in winter.
Cultivation: Plant 3ft (1m) apart when all danger of frost is past.
Aftercare: Grow indoors in winter in cold climates.
Harvest: Leaves when needed, but best when flowers begin to bloom.
USES:
Aromatic/decorative: Add dried leaves to potpourri, linen sachets, and herb pillows.
Cosmetic: Macerate leaves in almond oil to use as a massage. Infuse leaves to bathe eyes; add to bath water for a refreshing bath.
Culinary: Use finely chopped young leaves in apple jelly, cookies, dessert sauces, fruit puddings, and home-made ice creams.

Oregano (Origanum vulgare)
Hardy herbaceous perennial

Height/spread: 12 x 12in (30 x 30cm).
Description: Dark green, peppery leaves; pink or white flowers in summer.
Position: Sandy soil in sun or partial shade.
Cultivation: Sow indoors or in situ in spring; thin or plant out 12-18in (30-45cm) apart. Propagate by dividing in spring or fall.

Aftercare: Cut back hard in fall.
Harvest: Young leaves when needed; flower buds before they open.
USES:
Aromatic/decorative: Use dried flowers and leaves in herb pillows and potpourri.
Cosmetic: Add leaves to bath water; infuse for a hair conditioner.
Culinary: Add fresh or dried leaves or flower buds to Bolognaise sauce, cheese dishes, pizzas, roast lamb, salads, soups, and vegetable dishes. Use in bouquet garni.
Medicinal: Infuse leaves to treat coughs, nervous headaches, and menstrual pains.
❧ Oregano is attractive to bees and butterflies.

Oswego tea / Bergamot (Monarda didyma)
Hardy herbaceous perennial

Height/spread: 28 x 12in (70 x 30cm).
Description: Dark green, very aromatic leaves with red veins; red flowers in late summer.
Position: Rich, light, moist soil in partial shade.
Cultivation: Sow in spring; thin to 18in (45cm) apart. Propagate by dividing in spring or fall.
Aftercare: Mulch round plants in spring; cut back from time to time to keep plants within bounds.
Harvest: Leaves in spring or summer; flowers when fully open.
USES:
Aromatic/decorative: Add dried flowers and leaves to potpourri. Include flowers in fresh or dried arrangements.
Culinary: Add leaves and flowers to salads.
Medicinal: Infuse leaves to relieve insomnia, menstrual discomfort, and nausea.

Parsley (Petroselinum crispum)
Hardy biennial

Height/spread: 15 x 8in (40 x 20cm).
Description: Bright green, fresh-tasting leaves; tiny, yellowish green flowers in summer.
Position: Rich, moist soil in sun or partial shade.
Cultivation: Sow in spring in cool climates, in fall in warmer regions; thin to 9in (23cm) apart. Seeds can be slow to germinate—to speed things up, soak them in warm water overnight, or pour boiling water in the drills before sowing.
Aftercare: Cover in cold weather.
Harvest: Leaves from one-year-old plants.
USES:
Cosmetic: Infuse leaves for a hair tonic or eye bath.
Culinary: Add to broiled meats, fish sauces, salads, soups, and vegetable dishes. Use in bouquet garni.
Medicinal: Chew raw leaves to freshen breath; infuse for a diuretic and tonic.
❧ Parsley can be grown indoors.

PEPPERMINT (*Mentha x piperita*)
Hardy herbaceous perennial

Height/spread: 20-24 x 8in (50-60 x 20cm).
Description: Dark green, aromatic leaves on reddish stems; pinkish lilac flowers in summer.
Position: Rich, moist soil in partial shade.
Cultivation: Plant rooted runners in spring. Roots are very invasive and it is advisable to restrict them by growing plants in containers. Does not breed true from seed.
Aftercare: Clip regularly and keep well watered.
Harvest: Leaves when needed, but best just before plant flowers.
USES:
Aromatic/decorative: Add dried leaves to scented sachets and potpourri.
Culinary: Add leaves to carrots, fruit juices, fruit salads, and zucchini (courgettes).
Household/garden: Fresh or dried leaves repel ants and mice. Grow near roses to deter aphids.
Medicinal: Infuse leaves to relieve colds, flu, and indigestion and to stimulate appetite.

POT MARIGOLD (*Calendula officinalis*)
Hardy annual

Height/spread: 12-20 x 12in (30-50 x 30cm).
Description: Mid-green, slightly hairy leaves; golden yellow, or orange flowers in late spring, summer, and fall.
Position: Best in light, rich soil in sun, but will tolerate all but heavily waterlogged soils.
Cultivation: Sow in situ in spring; thin to 18-24in (45-60cm) apart. Self-seeds freely.
Aftercare: Deadhead to prolong flowering.
Harvest: Leaves when young; flowers when just fully open.
USES:
Aromatic/decorative: Dried petals add color to potpourri.
Cosmetic: Add petals to creams and lotions to cleanse and soften skin.
Culinary: Petals add delicate, saffron color to egg, cheese, and rice dishes. Add to butter, cakes, cookies, milk dishes, and yogurt.
Household/garden: Boil flowers to produce pale yellow dye.
Medicinal: Add flowers to ointments to treat leg ulcers and varicose veins. Infuse leaves to bathe tired feet.

ROSEMARY *(Rosemarinus officinalis)*
Hardy evergreen perennial

Height/spread: 3-6 x 6ft (1-2 x 2m).
Description: Grayish green, needlelike, aromatic leaves; small, pale blue flowers in spring.
Position: Poor, well-drained, alkaline soil in sun.
Cultivation: Sow indoors in spring. Plant out 24-36in (60-90cm) apart in summer. Propagate by layering, or take cuttings in late summer and plant out in spring.
Aftercare: Protect in winter in cold climates. Water sparingly.
Harvest: Cut small sprigs as needed, but flavor is best just before plants flower.
USES:
Aromatic/decorative: Add dried leaves to potpourri. Makes attractive, aromatic hedge.
Cosmetic: Add leaves to bath water; infuse for a facial steam for blackheads and a rinse for dark hair.
Culinary: Use with baked potatoes, halibut, lamb, and pork.
Household/garden: Boiled sprigs make effective disinfectant. Stems make fragrant barbecue skewers.
Medicinal: Infuse leaves to stimulate circulation.

Sage (Salvia officinalis)
Hardy evergreen shrub

Height/spread: 24-48 x 36in (60-120 x 90cm).
Description: Grayish green, downy, aromatic leaves; bluish mauve flowers in summer.
Position: Any well-drained soil in full sun.
Cultivation: Sow indoors in early spring; plant out 18in (45cm) apart in late spring.
Aftercare: Prune regularly. Replace plants every 4-5 years.
Harvest: Leaves just before plant flowers.
USES:
Cosmetic: Infuse leaves for facial steams, cleansing lotions, and mouthwash, and for a rinse to darken gray hair. Fresh leaves can be used to whiten teeth.
Culinary: Use with meat, poultry, soups, stews, and vegetable dishes. Add chopped leaves to stuffings.
Household/garden: Dried leaves deter insects.
Medicinal: Infuse leaves to aid digestion, and to make antiseptic mouthwash and hair conditioner.
❧ Sage can be grown indoors.

Thyme (Thymus vulgaris)
Hardy evergreen shrub

Height/spread: 12-18 x 24in (30-45 x 60cm).
Description: Small, green, aromatic leaves; small, pale lilac flowers in summer.
Position: Light, well-drained, alkaline soil in full sun.
Cultivation: Sow in situ in spring; thin to 15in (40cm) apart. Propagate by stem cuttings or division in spring.
Aftercare: Prune regularly. Protect in winter in cold climates.
Harvest: Leaves while plant is flowering.
USES:
Aromatic/decorative: Add dried flowers to potpourri. Makes attractive, low, aromatic hedge.
Cosmetic: Add leaves to bath water and facial steams and to ointments to treat spots.
Culinary: Use in bouquet garni. Add to marinades and stuffings, oils and vinegar.
Household/garden: Make decoction for an effective disinfectant.
Medicinal: Make tincture to use as mouthwash and gargle. Infuse leaves to aid digestion and alleviate hangovers.
~ Thyme can be grown indoors and in containers.

Medicinal: Infuse leaves to alleviate indigestion and to regulate menstruation. Chew leaf to relieve toothache. Make decoction to treat chapped skin, rashes, and wounds.

CHAPTER THREE

The Kitchen Garden

My first attempt at herb gardening was to grow a few sprigs of mint in a plastic flowerpot—I liked mint sauce, and found the idea of making my own quite exciting and adventurous. Encouraged by the success of my mint (and the sauce), I planted a few garlic cloves and some parsley in a patch of soil in the back yard and, pretty soon, I had what I considered to be a well-stocked little herb garden. When a friend suggested I might try growing some lavender and, perhaps, a few nasturtiums *(Tropaeolum majus)*, I patiently explained that I grew only "culinary" herbs, and "ornamental things" didn't qualify for a place in my plot.

What great injustice I was doing to the herbs–and to myself! In my innocence, I believed "culinary" to mean "for the cooking pot only." Any herb described otherwise might have its place somewhere, but that place was most certainly not in my kitchen garden; and the idea that any of my precious "culinary" herbs might be used for such things as fragrant baths and cough cures was quite unthinkable!

Some of the blame for my early misconceptions must surely lie with those compilers of herb catalogs and (dare I say it?) writers of gardening books, who seem unable to resist the temptation to categorize their subject matter in tidy little "boxes," with sage, for example, forever imprisoned in the one labeled "culinary herbs," and lavender similarly confined in the "ornamental" or "potpourri" box.

Culinary herbs are any herbs that you choose to use in the preparation of food, and the closer to the kitchen you can grow them, the better—the need to don rubber boots and trench coat to gather a few sprigs of parsley on a wet day is best avoided if possible.

The Back Yard Plot

*I*f you can spare a little land immediately outside the kitchen door, fill it with those herbs that you use most often. A patch a few feet (meters) square, or a sunny border at the foot of the house wall will accommodate "cut-and-come-again" herbs, such as chives, oregano, sage, parsley, rosemary, and thyme, and "dual purpose" ones, such as dill and coriander, that you need for leaves, rather than seeds. Plant the taller-growing herbs toward the back, where they won't cast shade on the others, and grow the parsley as a neat edging around the whole plot. If the border is too wide for the plants at the back to be accessible from the path, lay a few steppingstones here and there—use two or three bricks bedded into the soil side by side, or a few small paving stones, just large enough to accommodate your feet.

Herbs that are grown mainly for their roots, are best planted away from the main plot. Otherwise, lifting them could disturb the roots of the other herbs.

Grow the seed-producing herbs in clumps in other parts of the garden. They don't need to be close to the kitchen door, since you'll harvest and dry the seeds all at once, rather then collect them as you need them. Growing enough plants to provide seeds to last through the year will take up valuable space in the "cut-and-come again" plot.

Potagers

A potager, in the strictest sense of the word, is a formal, geometric, ornamental garden where herbs, fruit, and vegetables are grown together in a series of small beds, separated by grass or gravel paths. The design was originally created by the French as a means of growing a large quantity of mixed produce in a small space, but it is equally suitable for growing herbs.

Arrange the herbs in your potager in whatever way you find the most practical or pleasing. Plants whose foliage provides an interesting contrast of shape, color and texture can be grouped together, as can several varieties of the same species or those that are used mainly for the same purpose, such as medicinal herbs, or those for dyeing, or making potpourri. In the traditional potager, fruit trees and climbing vegetables, such as pole beans (climbing beans), provide a backdrop. In an herb potager the same effect can be achieved with trees and shrubs, such as elder *(Sambucus canadensis / S. nigra)* and the early flowering, sweetly scented witch hazel *(Hamamelis virginiana)*, combined with golden hops *(Humulus lupulus 'Aureus')* and fragrant honeysuckle *(Lonicera)*.

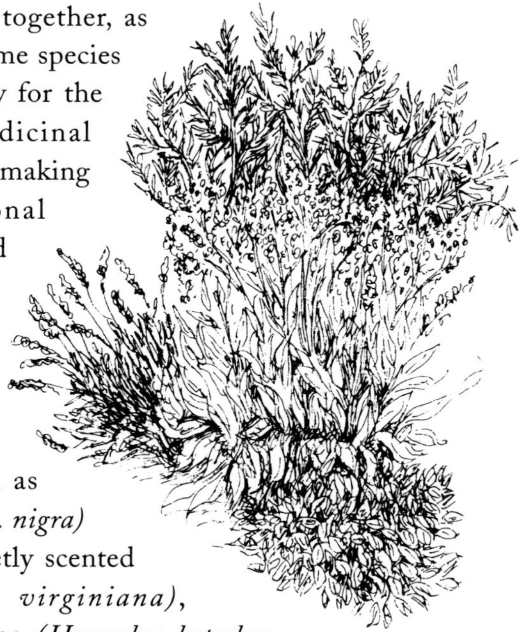

Herbs on the Patio

There is no better way to soften the effect of a large, flat expanse of brick or paving than by growing tiny, creeping herbs between the stones and surrounding the whole area with those that give off their heady aromas at the slightest touch. Plant some lavenders, sages and thymes in the borders around the seating area on your patio—your guests will be unable to resist the temptation to touch them while they sip their drinks on a sunny afternoon!

Hanging Baskets

Hanging baskets are ideal for smaller collections of herbs–try an assortment of mints with contrasting leaf colors and textures. Plant upright varieties, such as peppermint, spearmint, pineapple mint (M. *sauveolens* 'Variegata'), which has leaves with cream margins and white stems, eau-de-cologne mint (M. *x piperita* 'Citrata'), with bronze leaves, and gingermint (M. *x gracilis* 'Variegata') which has variegated green and yellow leaves, in the top of the basket, and creeping pennyroyal (M. *pulegium* 'Cunningham Mint') to trail down around the sides.

Herbs Indoors

Whether you have a garden or not, there is always a place for herbs inside the house. Pots of basil, mint, coriander, and parsley can be kept within easy reach on the windowsill and will fill the kitchen with their deliciously appetizing aromas. Eau-de-cologne mint and lavender will perfume a bathroom or cloakroom, and chamomile, with its soothing perfume, is perfect for a bedroom or nursery.

CHAPTER FOUR

The Ornamental Herb Garden

Formal and Informal Gardens

In contrast to the kitchen garden, where, of necessity, functionality often takes precedence over appearance, the ornamental herb garden affords the opportunity for the creativity of the gardener to play a major role. For some, the geometric balance of a formal garden, with straight paths, neatly clipped hedges, and elegant statuary is the ideal. For others, a more natural setting, where the plants are allowed to grow freely in a profusion of color and seed themselves with gay abandon, is the ultimate goal.

In the formal garden, each plant is grown in the way that best displays its individual beauty, much in the same way as a painting is hung to best advantage in an exhibition. The informal garden is like a collage, where a variety of colors and shapes are combined to create an overall effect.

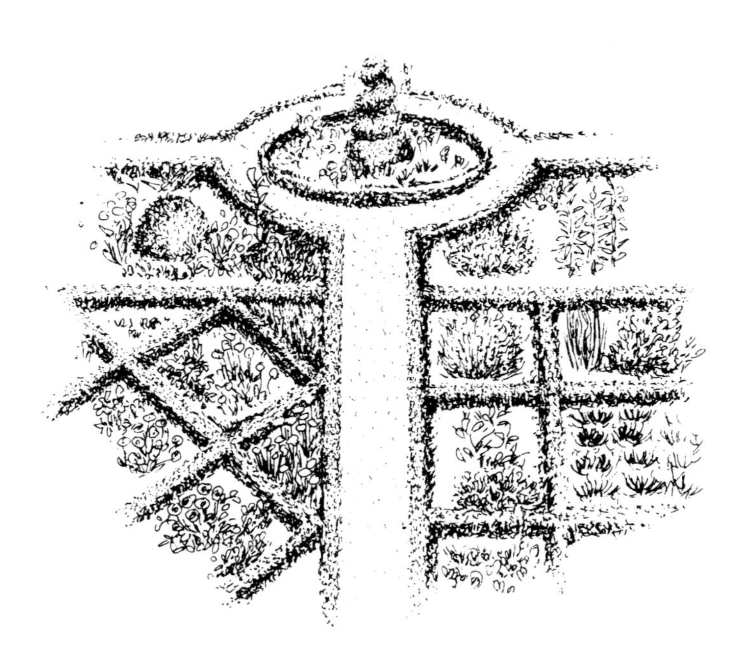

Beds and Borders

For maximum effect, herbs in informal beds and borders are best planted in groups of three or five of each species. As a general rule, plants, such as angelica, evening primrose, and fennel, that grow to a height of more than 36in (90cm) should be at the back, with those that stand between about 18in and 36in (50cm and 90cm)—borage, horehound, and rue (*Ruta graveolens*), for example, in the middle, and the short and creeping or trailing herbs, such as catnip, savory (*Satureja*), and thyme, at the front. However, keeping rigidly to this layout can result in a rather regimented look, and it is often more effective to allow a clump or two of medium-height plants to grow at the front.

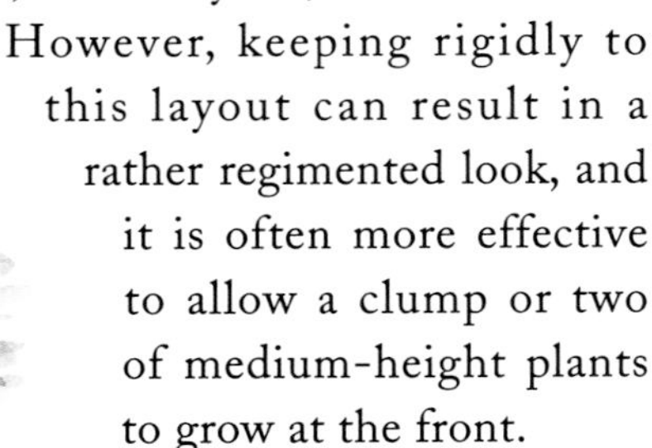

*I*sland beds, where the plants can been seen from all sides, should have the tallest in the center, with the shortest around the edges and the others in between.

In formal borders, the herbs can be planted in a bold, geometric pattern and the pattern repeated along the entire length of the border. In an area 16 x 4ft (5 x 1.2m), for example, you could accommodate four 4ft (1.2m) square patterns. The combinations of herbs that can be grown in this way are endless. Each pattern might consist of a sweet bay in a tub, or a species rose, such as the apothecary's rose, as a centerpiece, surrounded by a 2ft (60cm) diameter circle of, perhaps, rosemary, rue, or sage, with the circle enclosed in a 4ft (1.2m) square of dwarf boxwood (*Buxus sempervirens 'Suffruiticosa'*), clipped lavender, lavender cotton / cotton lavender (*Santolina*), or thyme.

Knot Garden

Knot gardens, those much-loved creations of Elizabethan England, require a good deal of maintenance if they are to look their best, but the time required to keep them trimmed is amply rewarded. The simplicity or complexity of the design is entirely a matter of personal preference, but it is always best to plan it on paper first. In a knot garden the herbs are enclosed by dwarf hedges, usually of boxwood or lavender, which are planted to create distinctive shapes, such as diamonds, stars, crosses, or even initials. Compact, hummock-forming herbs, such as lady's mantle, sweet or knotted marjoram (*Origanum majorana*), or English violets (*Viola odorata*), which are neither vigorous nor invasive, are the best types to grow in the "enclosures."

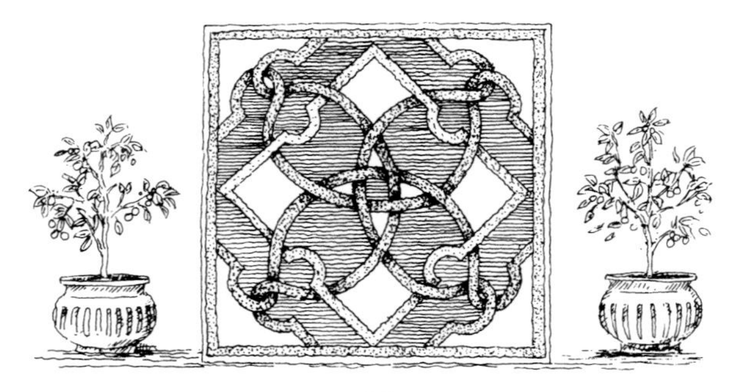

Raised Beds

There are advantages for both the plants and the gardener in growing in raised beds: if your garden soil is heavy clay, very chalky, or badly drained, you can provide ideal conditions for your herbs by constructing a series of raised beds and filling them with the type of soil best suited to their needs. These beds eliminate the need to bend or kneel in order to tend the plants, and are ideal for wheelchair-bound gardeners. For those with poor vision, who identify herbs primarily by their aroma, raised beds make the plants more accessible.

Construct the walls from bricks, stones, or even old railroad ties to a height and width that suits your needs. If the beds are to be filled with a different type of soil than that in the surrounding garden, it should be of sufficient depth to prevent the roots of the herbs from penetrating beyond the bottom of the bed—the roots of comfrey, for example, may go down as much as 3ft (1m). Provided you take this into account, you can grow all your herbs in raised beds.

Herb Wheels

Sadly, the demise of the horse and cart as a means of transport has made it almost impossible to find genuine wagon wheels today. Some garden centers may stock "reproduction" wheels, but often these are much smaller than the real thing and suitable for growing only a few small herbs. The best solution is to construct a large wheel shape from bricks or paving stones. Use a circular stone in the center for the hub, and make the rim and each of the spokes, wide enough to serve as paths. The hub can support either a containerized plant, such as a bay tree, or a standard rose; a piece of statuary, or a sundial or bird bath. Each segment of the wheel can accommodate several plants of the same herb, or may feature a variety of plants grouped together. Medium- to low-growing herbs are best, as very tall species may obscure the central feature.

Theme Gardens

A theme garden is one in which each plant is associated in some way with the others growing around it. The link may be practical, historical, cultural, or based on color, or, perhaps, on the plants' ability to attract bees and butterflies. The following are just a few of the many themes you could choose:

The Wildlife Garden: Basil, borage, catnip, comfrey, horehound, lavender, Oswego tea / bergamot, pot marigold, rosemary, sage, savory, sweet marjoram, and thyme.

The White Garden: Caraway, daisy (*Bellis perennis*), lavender cotton, lily of the valley (*Convallaria majalis*), sweet Cicely (*Myrrhis odorata*), wormwood (*Artemesia absinthium*), and Musk mallow (*Malva moschata*).

The Dyer's Garden: Ragwort (*Senecio jacobaea*) and tansy (*Tanacetum vulgare*) for yellow dyes, elder and sorrel (*Rumex acetosa*) for greens, madder (*Rubia tinctorum*) for orange, and woad (*Isatis tinctoria*) for blue.

The Native American Garden: Horsetail (*Equisetum arvense*), Oswego tea / bergamot, sweet gale (*Myrica gale*), and wild rose (*Rosa canina*).

The Shakespearean Garden: Bay, borage, columbine (*Aquilegia vulgaris*), eglantine (*Rosa eglanteria*), lady's smock (*Cardamine pratensis*), lavender, thyme, and woodbine (*Lonicera periclymenum*).

Statuary

The plants in my formal herb garden grow under the watchful eye of Pan, the Greek god of shepherds and their flocks. He peeps through the foliage and adds an almost magical quality to the garden. He is not large, nor was he expensive, but my little plot would not be the same without him.

A statue can act as a focal point in the garden, leading the eye in a particular direction. Strategically placed, it can help to create the illusion of length in a short garden or width in a narrow one.

Choose your garden ornaments with care. Always try to match the period of the statue with the style of the garden. Size is important too; if the statue is too small for its surroundings, it will be lost; one that is too large will overpower and look incongruous.

Most garden ornaments are made from concrete, bronze, marble, stone, or terra-cotta, and are priced accordingly. If you live in a cooler region, make sure that anything made of terra-cotta is guaranteed frostproof. If the label says "frost-resistant," be prepared to protect the item in winter—a sudden hard frost may cause irreparable damage.

It can take some years for concrete or reconstituted stone ornaments to "age" and lose their stark, white appearance. Placing the ornament in a damp, shady place will speed up the process by encouraging algae to grow. For more instant results, paint the surface with a mixture of one part yogurt to ten parts water.

CHAPTER FIVE
Growing Herbs

Planning and Preparing the Site

The first step in creating a herb garden is deciding which herbs you want to grow. Gardening books and catalogs, however detailed and well illustrated, can provide only the most basic information. While it is easy for most of us to visualize a plant described as being 3ft (1m) tall, with grayish green leaves, for example, words cannot conjure up the sensation of touching those leaves or of smelling their fragrance.

Before making your final decision on what to grow, visit a herb nursery or garden center, or, better still, one of the many herb gardens that are open to the public. There, you can touch and smell the plants and compare different planting schemes.

When you have decided which herbs you want to grow, make a list. Include notes on the final height and spread of each herb and the growing conditions it prefers, and whether it is annual, biennial, or perennial. When the list is complete and you have decided on the style of garden you want to create, it's time to put aside the gardening books and catalogs and get out the tools.

The first things you will need are a long tape measure, a note pad, a pencil, ruler, eraser and several sheets of graph paper. If you can persuade a friend to lend a hand by taking charge of one end of the tape measure, then so much the better.

Begin by measuring the length and width of the plot, and make a rough sketch on the note pad. Measure the sizes and positions of any existing features, such as trees, sheds, greenhouses, and paths, that you intend to keep and mark them on the sketch, along with the points of the compass in relation to your garden. Note which areas receive the most sun, and those that are in shade for all, or a large part of the day. If there are any places where the soil is badly drained or very stony, or places that are exposed to high winds or likely to become frost pockets in winter, mark them too.

When the sketch is complete, draw it to scale on the graph paper, transferring your notes as you go, then add any new, permanent features, such as arches, pergolas, or paths, that you intend to construct.

*I*f your herbs are to flourish, they should be grown in conditions as close as possible to those in which they grow in the wild—periwinkle *(Vinca)* and woodruff *(Galium odoratum)*, for example, are plants of moist, shady woodlands, and will not do well if you plant them on a sun-scorched rockery. Mediterranean herbs, such as marjoram and thyme, however, whose natural habitats are rocky, south-facing hillsides, will perform best in just such a position.

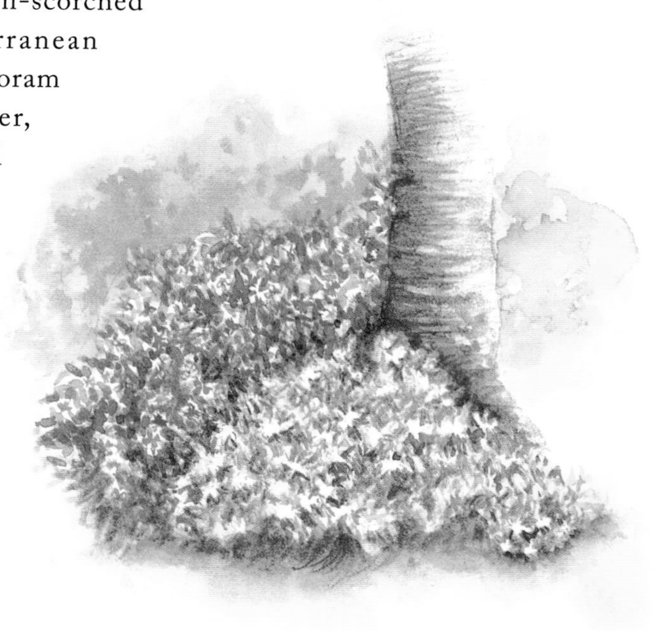

The moisture level of the soil, and the right amount of sun or shade are more important to most herbs than is the pH level of the soil in which they are grown. Soil with a pH of 7 is neutral (neither alkaline nor acid). Most herbs will grow happily in soil with a pH of between 6.5 (slightly acid) and 7.5 (slightly alkaline). Among the exceptions are rosemary, which needs an alkaline soil and mint which does best in an acid one.

Garden centers sell kits, which are cheap and easy to use, for testing the pH level of soil. Always test separate samples from different parts of the garden. Even in a small garden, the pH levels can vary from place to place. If your soil is acidic (below pH 6.5), regular applications of Dolomitic lime will gradually raise the pH. Reducing the alkalinity of soils over 7.5 is a little more difficult–digging in large quantities of well-rotted manure may help, but too much manure can have a detrimental effect on many herbs, particularly Mediterranean ones, whose production of essential oils is severely reduced if they are grown in rich soil. The best solution is to grow lime-hating herbs in raised beds filled with neutral or slightly acid soil.

If the pH level of the soil in your garden varies from place to place, make a note of this on your plan then, with all the information to hand, you can begin to allocate your chosen herbs to the parts of the garden which best suit their needs. If your list includes invasive herbs such as mints, remember to make provision on your plan for containers or separate beds where you can keep them controlled more easily.

*U*se colored pencils or crayons to sketch in the herbs on the plan, especially if color combinations are to be a major consideration in your design. Experiment with different combinations and designs until you find the ones you like best. When you are satisfied with the overall effect, try to resist the temptation to rush into the garden to make a start. Instead, pin your plan to a wall near a window that overlooks the garden and leave it there for a few days. Study it from time to time and try to visualize it as a reality in the garden. You will almost certainly find small things that you would like to change or improve.

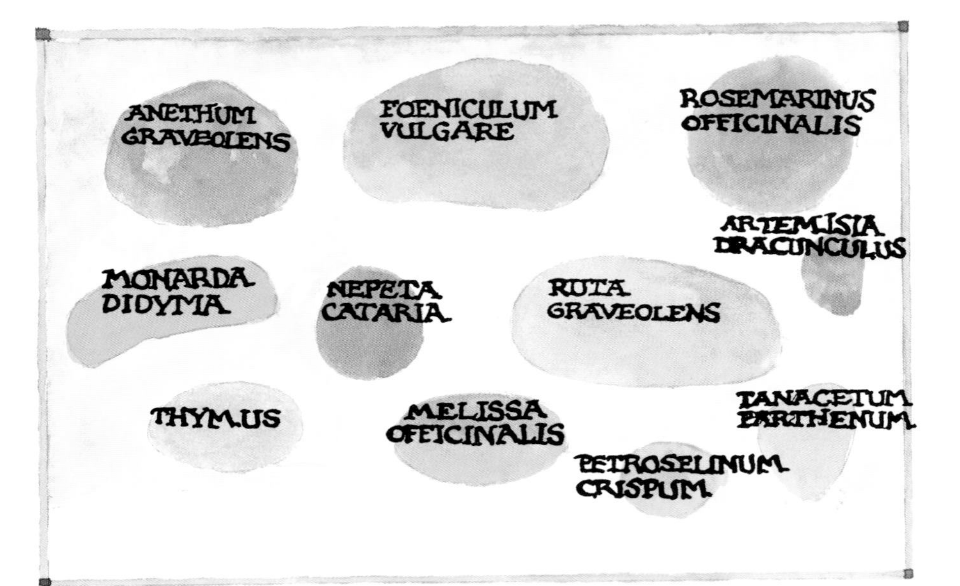

In the meantime, dig up and dispose of any plants that you no longer want and clear the garden of any trash. If your plan includes paths, walls, archways, and the like, calculate what materials you will need and order them from suppliers, or pick them up in person at your garden center. Don't buy the plants until the garden is ready to receive them.

Gardening should always be a pleasure—never a chore. Before you even open the garden shed, make yourself a resting place in the garden. Bring out a comfortable chair and set it in a shady place, or sling a hammock between two trees. Put some beers or soft drinks in the fridge to chill (next summer, you could be drinking iced mint tea!), and decide where you want to begin. If you have a camera, you might like to take a few photographs of the garden each time you make a change. In years to come, when the garden is well established and flourishing, you'll experience a great sense of achievement remembering how it once was.

When I moved to my present house about fifteen years ago, there wasn't a bare patch of soil to be seen in the garden—a shoulder-high forest of weeds made sure of that! Today, the enjoyment I get from looking at the photographs of how it was and tracing the changes that have made it what it is now, is almost as great as the enjoyment I get from the garden itself.

When you are ready to begin transferring your plan to the garden, you'll need some string and some pegs to mark out the positions of the beds, paths, walls, and anything else that will eventually create the framework for your plants. Work on one section at a time and take lots of breaks in your seat, or hammock in the shade—there's no hurry—making a garden is something to be enjoyed at leisure.

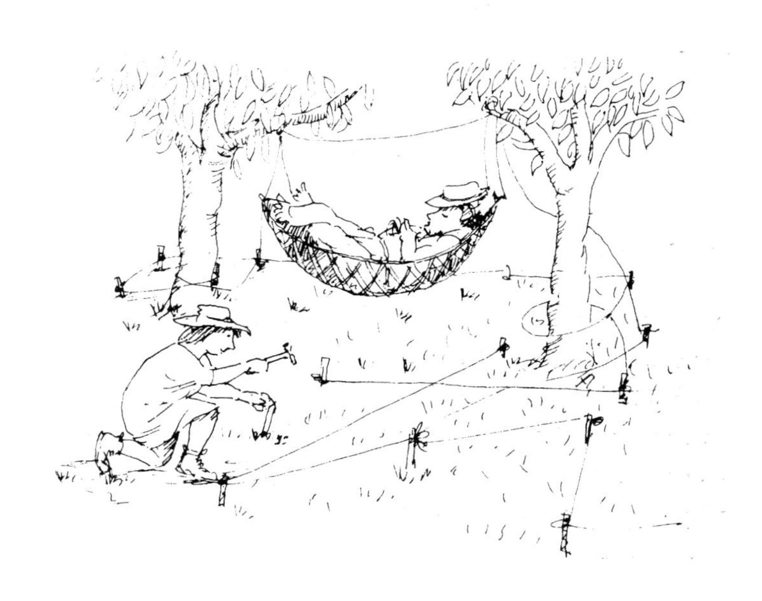

When you do begin spading, you must remove the roots of pernicious weeds, such as couch and bindweed. Any small fragments of these that remain will grow and spread, and once the plants are in place, will be impossible to eradicate. As I, and countless other gardeners have learned from experience, complete removal of these roots is easier said than done. Spading or tilling can often make matters worse by chopping up unseen roots and spreading them through the soil.

After many years of using a spade in a vain attempt to beat back the ever-advancing armies of weeds in my garden, I decided to change tactics and starve them into submission instead. I spread some old carpet over the soil and left it in place for a year. Total light-deprivation proved fatal to the weeds, and the part of my land that I covered has been reclaimed from the invaders. Although this method takes a while, the results are worth waiting for and it saves many hours of labor.

When you have done the spading and weeding spread a thin layer of well-rotted compost over the soil and turn it into the top 2-3in (5-8cm) with a garden fork—digging it in more deeply puts it out of reach of the plants' roots. Don't add compost where you intend to grow herbs that need poor soil, such as anise and nasturtiums. For herbs that prefer a rich soil, you can, if you like, apply a little balanced organic fertilizer, such as fish, blood, and bone meal, in addition to the compost.

Leave the soil to settle for a week or two and, in the meantime, buy your chosen herbs from a garden center or order them from a mail-order catalog or herb nursery. Always unpack mail-order plants as soon as they arrive, and check them carefully for damage, or signs of pests or diseases on the foliage and the roots—a reputable supplier should be prepared to replace any plant that is not satisfactory.

The best time to plant herbs is in the evening or on a cool, overcast day. Water the pots well and leave them to drain, then refer to your original plan. Set the pots in position on top of the soil, leaving the appropriate amount of space between each, according to its final spread. Use a trowel to dig a hole just large enough to accommodate the root-ball, then upend the pot and tap the bottom with the trowel. Remove the plant gently and pop it in the hole. Fill any gaps with soil and firm it down well, then water the plant generously to settle the soil around its roots. Make a label, written in indelible ink, for each plant and push it into the soil close to the stem. Your herb garden is now a reality and, given a little initial care and attention, it should help to keep you healthy and happy for many years to come.

Planting Containers and Baskets

*I*f possible, site the container in its final position before you begin to fill it. Alternatively, stand it on a small trolley (a piece of board with a wheel at each corner will do) or in a wheel barrow, and wheel it to its destination once it is planted. If a large container is to stand somewhere that requires it to be carried up a flight of stairs, always position it before you fill it.

The basic ingredients are the same for all containers. You will need shards of crockery to cover the holes in the base (pieces of broken terra-cotta flowerpots are ideal), gravel to cover the bottom of the container to a depth of about 1-2in (2.5-5cm), potting mix to fill the container to about 2in (5cm) below its rim, and the plants. You can buy potting mix at garden centers, but read the labels carefully to make sure you are getting what you need. Potting mix for herbs, particularly herbs for culinary and medicinal use, should be free of chemical fertilizers. For herbs that are intolerant of alkaline soil, it should also be lime-free.

Water the herbs well and leave them to drain while you prepare the container. Cover each drainage hole with a piece of crockery, then add a 2in (5cm) layer of gravel. Add potting mix until the level is high enough for the top of the soil round the plants to be about 2in (5cm) below the rim of the container. If the herbs are in pots of varying depths, plant those from the deepest pots first. Fill in with more potting mix to raise the level, then plant the others. Water the completed container well and allow it to drain, then top up with more potting mix if necessary.

Hanging baskets come in a variety of designs, ranging from the wire-mesh type, which needs a liner, to plastic containers made in the traditional basket shape, but with only one drainage hole in the bottom. Some have an integral drip tray. These need no liners and can be planted up in the same way as other containers.

To plant in a wire basket, you will need a liner. Traditionally, baskets were lined with sphagnum moss, but the world's resources of this material are becoming severely depleted and many very satisfactory substitutes, such as coconut fiber or synthetic moss, are widely available. You will also need a circular piece of plastic large enough to completely cover the inside of the liner, a handful of gravel, potting mix to fill the basket to about 1in (2.5cm) below the rim (special, soilless mixes are available which are lighter in weight than the mixes for containers), and the plants.

As with containers, the quantity of potting mix you need depends on the size of the basket and the amount of soil on the roots of the plants. As a rough guide, a basket 14in (35cm) in diameter will hold about 2 3/4 gallons (ten liters).

Stand the basket on top of a pail or large flowerpot, and insert the liner, smoothing it carefully so that the top protrudes about 1in (2.5cm) above the rim of the basket. Cut a couple of slits in the circular piece of plastic, fit it inside the liner, then add the gravel, followed by a 3in (7.5cm) layer of potting mix. Cut holes through both liners just above the level of the potting mix for any herbs that are to grow down from the sides of the basket. Remove these herbs from their pots and insert the roots carefully from the outside of the basket (you may have to bend the wires a little to increase the size of the holes), making sure their roots come into contact with the potting mix. If you have difficulty pushing the roots through the holes, put each plant, root first, into a plastic bag before you insert it. Remove the bag once the plant is in place. Add a little more potting mix to the basket and firm it gently around the roots, then plant the remaining herbs in the top of the basket, beginning in the center and working outward. Water well, leave to drain, then add more potting mix if you need to. Fold the top 1in (2.5cm) of liner over the rim of the basket to form a collar, or trim it off neatly if you prefer.

Aftercare

Once established, most herbs, whether they are grown in the garden or in containers, require only a minimum amount of attention. Until they have settled into their new surroundings and are showing signs of new, healthy growth, keep the soil clear of weeds and water frequently the ones that need damp conditions. Water less often those that prefer drier conditions. Containerized herbs will need watering more regularly than those growing in the garden.

Annual weeds can be a problem even in established gardens, but regular hoeing between the herbs will dispose of the weeds while they are still at the seedling stage. Alternatively, you can spread a 2-3in (5-7.5cm) deep layer of pulverized bark or gravel around and between the plants. This will keep all but the most persistent weeds at bay.

A light mulch of well-rotted compost, applied to the soil once a year in spring or fall, is all that most herbs need to keep them growing vigorously. Overfeeding, with either compost or fertilizer, leads to too much sappy growth, makes the plants vulnerable to attacks by pests and diseases, and reduces their production of essential oils. This, in turn, reduces their medicinal, culinary, and aromatic properties.

Propagation

Many annual herbs self-seed freely. Others, the mints, for example, propagate themselves by throwing up shoots from root runners. These seedlings and shoots never grow just where you want them, but you can lift and transplant them to increase your stock.

Collect the seeds of less-prolific herbs and sow them, either in situ in mid- to late spring, of the following year, or in flats (seed trays) indoors in early spring. Always sow seeds of herbs, such as anise, coriander, dill, and parsley, which do not transplant successfully, directly into the soil. Angelica seeds lose their viability if they are stored, and they should be sown in late summer as soon as they are harvested.

When you sow in flats, scatter small seeds thinly over the surface of the potting mix and sprinkle a very fine layer of the mix on top. For larger seeds, make small holes $^1/_2$ -1in (1-2.5cm) apart with a knitting needle. As a rule of thumb, seeds should be sown at a depth roughly equal to their diameter. Water the flats gently, label them, and cover with a sheet of glass. Cover the glass with a piece of old newspaper to keep out the light, then put the flats in a warm, dark place.

As soon as the seedlings appear, uncover the flats and move them to a well-lit place out of direct sunlight. When the seedlings are large enough to handle, thin them out or pot them up into 3in (8cm) pots and leave them to grow on. Harden them off for a week or two before you plant them out.

Propagation from Cuttings

Shrubby herbs, such as bay, lavender, and thyme, are best propagated from cuttings or by layering. They can be grown from seeds, but it can take several years for them to reach a reasonable size.

Take cuttings in mid- to late summer. Gently pull a few stems, each about 3in (7.5cm) long, from the parent plant. Trim the leaves from the lower third of the stems and insert the stems, up to the remaining leaves, round the edge of a 3in (7.5cm) pot filled with a combination of potting mix, and sharp sand. Water well and cover with a plastic bag, taking care that the bag doesn't touch the cuttings. Leave the pot in a warm, shady place, and water just enough to prevent the soil from drying out completely. By the following spring, the cuttings should show signs of new growth. Remove the bag, harden off the plants, then plant them out.

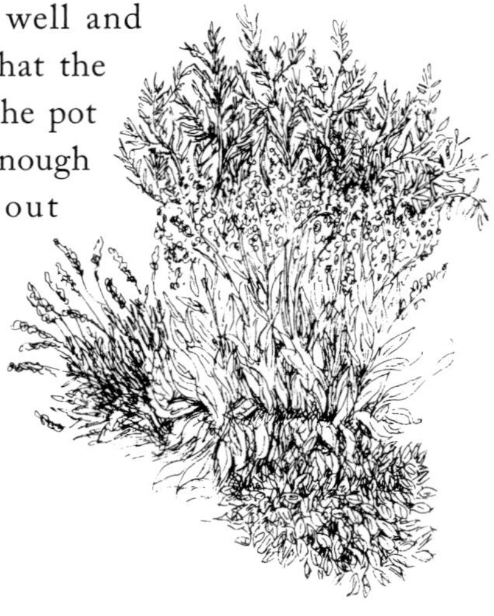

Propagating by Layering

To propagate by layering, peg down a few of the lower stems of the plant, making sure they come into close contact with the soil. Leave them undisturbed until the following spring, by which time they should have rooted. Use a sharp knife to separate the rooted stems from the parent plant, then dig them up and transplant them.

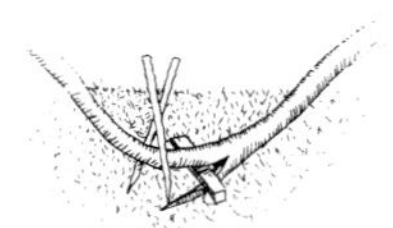

Propagating by Dividing

Hardy herbaceous perennial herbs and those with bulbous roots are best propagated by dividing. In the fall or early spring, while the plant is dormant, dig it up and separate the root into sections. If the root is very woody, insert two garden forks, back to back, in the center of the root mass, then gently ease it apart. Select the youngest, healthiest root sections and replant them immediately.

Pests and Diseases

Using chemical sprays on herbs grown for medicinal and culinary use is extremely unwise, and should be avoided at all costs. Even "organic" insecticides, such as derris and pyrethrum, although described as "safe" and "environmentally friendly," remain active on the plant for twenty-four hours. They are harmful to some beneficials, such as ladybugs (ladybirds), and extremely toxic to fish and other cold-blooded creatures. If you use these "safe" sprays, don't harvest the plants for at least two days, and wash them thoroughly.

The essential oils in herbs are natural insect repellents and bactericides, and some herbs, as well as having their own built-in resistance to attack, are also beneficial to their neighbors. If you keep your herb garden free of weeds and debris, the plants, for the most part, will take care of themselves and each other. Chamomile is known as "the plants' physician" because of its ability to repel flying insects. If you have a problem with ants, plant pennyroyal near their nests and you'll soon see the ants scuttling off in the opposite direction. Nasturtiums can help to repel whiteflies, and nettles can control blackflies. Grow sage and rosemary side by side, and each will help the other to flourish.

The more beneficial insects you can entice into the garden, the better. Grow dill and fennel to attract hoverflies, whose larvae prey on aphids, and southernwood to provide a breeding place for ladybugs. Biological control agents are also beneficial. You can buy them by mail order or from good garden centers and instructions for how to use them are given on the packs. If you grow herbs in containers, the parasitic nematode (*Heterohabditis megidis)* will ward off attacks by the larvae of the vine weevil.

*I*n hot, dry weather, mildew may attack some herbs, especially Oswego tea, sage, and thyme. It appears as a gray, powdery coating on the leaves, and is unsightly rather than fatal. Spraying vulnerable plants every evening with clean water will help to prevent attack.

The most difficult disease to deal with is rust. This is a fungus that attacks mints and causes brown blotches on the leaves. Unfortunately, the only successful way to eradicate it is to dig up and burn the infected plants. Plant new, healthy plants in another part of the garden, or in fresh potting mix in clean containers.

CHAPTER SIX

Harvesting and Storing

Few things are more satisfying than the sight of herbs drying in bunches hung from the kitchen ceiling or an old clothes airer. It is always worthwhile growing enough decorative and aromatic plants to provide some for drying this way. In the dark days of winter their subtle fragrance will recall the heady scents of the summer garden and hold out promises of the pleasures to come in the season ahead.

Every winter, I decorate my kitchen with bunches of herbs, and when the first rays of spring sunshine illuminate their faded colors, it is not without a twinge of sadness that I bid farewell to my once-beautiful decorations and turn them over to the compost worms—but, all is not lost–my pantry and freezer conceal sufficient supplies of herbs to last until the next harvest, the medicine chest holds tinctures and lotions to keep the family healthy, and assorted seeds in carefully labeled little packets occupy a corner of the salad compartment in the fridge. Soon it will be time to sow them, and a new growing season will have begun.

All herbs, except those for display in hanging bunches, should be laid out to dry in single layers. Spread them out, on slatted shelves if possible, in a well-ventilated, warm, dark place. Never attempt to dry them in a room where the temperature may fluctuate or where vapor gathers.

Always choose a warm, dry day for harvesting, and do it in the morning when the dew has evaporated but before the sun has risen too high in the sky. Gather leaves before the flower buds have opened, flowering tops when the buds have opened just enough to show a little color, and flowers as soon as they are open fully.

Examine seedheads every day once the seeds begin to ripen. When a gentle tap on the stem knocks a few seeds to the ground, cover the seedhead carefully with a paper bag, secure it with a piece of string tied just below the top of the stem, then cut down the plant and hang it upside down in a warm, well-ventilated place. As the seeds dry they will drop into the bag.

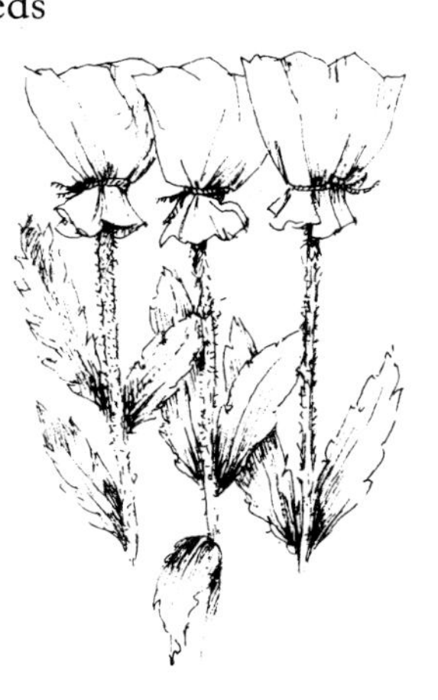

Harvest roots when the plant is dormant. Dig them up carefully, remove only as much as you will need, then replant the rest. Unlike the aerial parts of the plant, which should be washed only if absolutely necessary, roots must be scrubbed thoroughly and dried on paper towels. Slice the cleaned roots into usable portions, then lay them out to dry.

Dry thick-stemmed flowers for floral arrangements by standing them upright. Cut them close to the bases of their stems, as soon as the flowers have opened fully, then lay a piece of chicken wire over the top of a cardboard carton and insert one stem into each hole.

You can gather lavender easily and quickly if you gently grasp several stems at a time in one hand, then use a sawing action with a sharp knife held in the other hand to cut through the stems, just above the leaves. Lay the lavender out, if you have the space, or hang it upside down in small bunches.

Always gather only one herb at a time, and never harvest so much that you have neither the space nor the time to lay out all you have collected. Keep different aromatic herbs well away from one another—their aromas will mingle if they are dried together, and all the plants will be spoiled.

As soon as the herbs are brittle, but still green, they must be stored in airtight containers to prevent them from absorbing moisture from the atmosphere. If you want to display them on a kitchen shelf, use dark-colored glass jars with screw-top lids or earthenware containers with tightly fitting lids or corks, and stand them out of direct sunlight. Dried herbs deteriorate quickly when exposed to light, so if your containers are transparent, store them in a dark place. When the leaves are dry, remove them carefully from their stems to avoid crushing them. The more intact the leaves remain, the better they will retain their aromas and flavors. They can be crumbled as you need them.

If space is limited, you can dry small quantities of some herbs in a microwave or a very cool oven with the door open. Don't dry culinary herbs this way if you can avoid it, as it may spoil their flavors. Microwaves can alter the therapeutic properties of medicinal herbs, and they should never be dried this way.

Freezing is an excellent way to preserve herbs for culinary use, especially those, such as chives, coriander leaves, and parsley, that lose much of their flavor and color in the drying process. Put small bunches into freezer bags, seal and label them, then freeze in the usual way. Frozen herbs crumble easily and you can add them straight to the cooking pot when you need them, without defrosting them. Alternatively, chop the herbs finely and freeze them in ice-cube trays. When you are making soups, stews, and sauces, throw some cubes straight into the pot. Borage flowers or single mint leaves frozen in ice cubes add a pretty finishing touch to cold drinks.

CHAPTER SEVEN

Using Herbs

My husband, who is a very adventurous cook, once created a culinary masterpiece by experimenting with an assortment of herbs from the pantry. The praises of this "work of art" are still sung far and wide by our dinner guests of the day, but, unfortunately, I can't give you the recipe for this wonderful dish. This is not because the cook wishes the contents of his creation to remain a closely guarded secret, but because, in the heat of the moment (and the kitchen), we both neglected to write down what went into the skillet. Sadly, the ingredients of "Dan's Steak Surprise" will remain a mystery forever!

Whether you are cooking up a special dish, making a cup of tea, or assembling the ingredients for a fragrant herb pillow, always be prepared to experiment. Tried and tested recipes are good places to begin, but there is a whole world of herbs beyond minted peas, chamomile tea and hop pillows. Be adventurous—use your herbs in whatever combinations take your fancy, and enjoy to the full the wonderful, versatile plants you have grown—but whatever you make, remember to write down the recipe as you go.

Some Culinary Delights

Butters and cheeses: Beat together 3-5 tablespoons of chopped, fresh herbs, and 1 cup (225g) of unsalted butter or soft cheese at room temperature. Add a little lemon juice if you like, then chill.

Candied flowers and leaves: Dip each flower or leaf into lightly beaten egg, then into caster sugar. Shake off the excess sugar, and spread the flowers or leaves on a sheet of wax paper on a wire cooling rack. Cover with a second sheet of wax paper and put the tray into a heated closet or a very cool oven with the door open. When the flowers or leaves are dry, store them in an airtight tin.

Oils: Chop enough fresh herbs to loosely fill a clear-glass, screw-topped jar. Add oil (virgin olive oil is best) to cover the herbs completely, then screw the lid on tightly. Stand the jar on a sunny windowsill and shake it gently every day. After two weeks, strain the oil through cheesecloth or a fine nylon sieve into a clean container–discard the herbs onto the compost heap. Taste the oil—if you want a stronger flavor, repeat the process using more of the same herbs. Pour the flavored oil into a pretty glass bottle, add a sprig of the herb for decoration, cork tightly, and label.

Vinegars: Add two sprigs of your chosen herb to a bottle of red, or white wine vinegar, and stand it on a sunny windowsill. After two weeks, remove and discard the herb sprigs and replace with two more. The vinegar is then ready to use. To make garlic vinegar, add four peeled garlic cloves to the bottle, with or without the herbs, and leave for two weeks before using. There is no need to remove the garlic.

The Medicine Chest

Decoctions: To make one cupful, put 1 teaspoon of dried herbs (3 teaspoons fresh) into a stainless steel or enamel saucepan (do not use a copper or aluminum pan), and add 2 cups of cold water. Bring to a boil, then reduce the heat, cover, and simmer until the liquid has been reduced by half. Set aside for 3 minutes, then strain and serve, sweetened with a little honey or brown sugar, if you like.

Infusions (teas): Always use a warmed earthenware or china teapot, never a metal one. Put 1-2 teaspoons of dried herbs per cup (3-6 teaspoons fresh) into the pot and add boiling water. Cover and leave to stand for 3-5 minutes, then strain and serve, sweetened to taste.

"Green Tea" for Babies: This is a safe and gentle remedy to cure colic. Crush 1/2 teaspoon of anise, caraway, or dill seeds in a mortar and pestle. Put them into a small, warmed teapot, and pour in 1 cup of boiling water. Cover the pot and leave for 2-3 minutes, then strain the liquid into a clean container. Cover the container and allow the tea to stand until it is lukewarm, then pour it into baby's bottle.

Macerations: Put the fresh herbs into a bowl. For every 1oz (25g) of herbs add 2 cups (16 fl loz / 500ml) of cold water. Cover the bowl and leave the herbs to steep for at least 12 hours. Strain the liquid and use in the same way as infusions and decoctions.

Tinctures: For every 4oz (125g) of dried herbs (double the quantity for fresh), you will need 3 cups (25fl oz / 750ml) of pure alcohol, or 80 proof vodka. Put the herbs into a screw-top jar, add the alcohol, and cover tightly. Set in a warm, dark place, and shake vigorously twice daily. After 2 weeks, strain the tincture through cheesecloth or a fine nylon sieve. Squeeze the herbs to extract as much tincture as possible, then discard them onto the compost heap. Bottle, seal, and label the tincture, and store in a dark place.

Compresses: To make a hot compress, soak a piece of clean linen or cotton in a herbal decoction or infusion. Squeeze gently to remove excess liquid, then apply to the skin. Make cold compresses in the same way, but allow the decoction or infusion to cool completely before you soak the material.

Cough Syrups: Make an infusion and leave it to cool. To each cupful of liquid add 4 tablespoons of sugar. Bring to the boil, stirring constantly until the sugar has dissolved, then reduce the heat and simmer for 20 minutes until thickened.

Poultices: Crush the fresh herbs then mix them to a paste with a little boiling water. Apply to the skin, and cover with a piece of clean linen or cotton. The poultice should be hot, but not scalding. Remember that a child's skin is more sensitive than an adult's.

A Scented Sensation

Potpourri: In a bowl, mix together fragrant, dried flower petals and leaves, then stir in a fixative, such as ground orrisroot, which you can buy from health-food stores. Add some spices—ground or whole—and a few drops of essential oil. Cover the bowl with a tightly fitting lid, or wrap it in plastic wrap (cling film) and leave it in a warm, dark place. Shake the bowl gently from time to time. After about six weeks the potpourri will be ready to put on display.

Published by MQ Publications Limited
25–258 Goswell Road, London EC1V 7RL

ISBN: 1 84072 136 7

1 3 5 7 9 8 6 4 2

Printed and bound in Italy